Understories

Understories

Poems by

Peter Schireson

Cover design by Shay Culligan
Cover image by Simon Berger
Author photo by Patricia Amador

ISBN: 979-8-90146-821-0

Kelsay Books
502 South 1040 East, A-119
American Fork, Utah 84003
Kelsaybooks.com

for my Palm Springs poetry friends,
The Wordkeepers

Also by Peter Schireson

The Welter of Me and You

The Salt

Sword of Glass

What Worlds and Moons

How We Met

Before the Sun

Zen Bridge (co-editor)

Acknowledgments

The following poems in this volume have been published previously, sometimes in slightly different versions.

Apricity: "Beach"

Gyroscope Review: "Seaward"

Nine Mile Magazine: "Once, in a Small Patch of Sky"

Obsessed with Pipework: "As If the Dead Were Lurking Nearby"

Pinhole Poetry: "Report from the Afterlife"

The Poetry Lighthouse: "Goodbye, Ice Cream," "Kismet"

Stone Poetry Quarterly: "Art Supplies," "Universal Instructions"

Contents

My theory 13
Seaward 14
Productivity 15
The Purpose of Suffering 16
Backyard 17
Wavelength 18
The Hero Becomes Acquainted with the
Vagaries of Things 20
Necrophilous 22
Universal Instructions 23
Postures of Waking Up 25
Goodbye, Ice Cream 27
Biding, Abiding 28
The Abyss 29
Enlightenment 30
Once, in a Small Patch of Sky 32
Coco Is at Home 34
Balancing Act 35
Between the Stones 36
Dirt Road 38
Kismet 39
Chiaroscuro 40
The Week in Review 42
As if the Dead Were Lurking Nearby 44
Report from the Afterlife 45

My theory

is that every poem must find a way to prevail
over the commotion and ache in the darkness
and the attendant feeling of helplessness.
The darkness is a generous space—
birds sing in the branches as the trees burn,
mother and father, long dead, call out,
Chuck's car idles in a closed garage,
and you can smell the leaf-rot
as the earth makes ready.
So I look for a light switch,
or some form of comfort food to clear my head,
and usually I do find something,
mac and cheese, for example—
a holding action, not perfect,
but I think the poem depends on it.

Seaward

Accompanied by Thelonious Monk
and a small glass of bourbon,
I float out into the silver mist
that hangs over the yard.

Yellowed trees lean together like a band tuning up.
Perched on a twig, a finch chirps,
and is still, a conspiracy of beauty

in which I become an empty boat
drifting away on the warm shadow of a summer night,
impatience, yearning, bitterness, failure,
all drifting away.

Next morning, I try to pry that moment open—
was it just the bourbon and Monk, or was it a taste
of something like what religious people mean
when they talk about grace?

I join my wife in the kitchen,
the room honeyed with morning sun,
the air suffused with the healing fragrance of waffles.

We take our coffee back out to the yard.
Across the street, a teen girl walks a tiny dog
  on a rhinestone leash.
A dove pecks for worms at the edge of the grass.

Productivity

This morning, I planned
to get so many things done,

but I find myself just standing here leaning
against the shovel handle,

a man deep
in the grey season,

an eye-blink, leaning
and watching the dry grass rustle and incline,

as the larger world veers further and further
away.

The Purpose of Suffering

Every morning, I am slower.
It takes more and more time
to become myself.
Nights, a tiny squeaking
from somewhere in my body.
A dream of the sea,
falling, rising, wakes me.
On the nightstand in a shaft of moonlight,
a photograph of my three granddaughters.

Backyard

I have nothing that could qualify as actual knowledge about my backyard.

At the end of a long day, I sit in it. The afternoon, luminous, perfumed, evokes eternity. Everywhere birds' nests, and from the street, the untamed laughter of young girls. Sometimes, a no-man's-land made of anxiety, sometimes, a kind of menace, occasionally . . . grace.

Sitting like this in my backyard induces a seductive fever. A warm slow-moving breeze, the palms sway, testimony to primordial life. Language vanishes, only a ghost lingering in my mouth.

My dog trots out from the house, licks my hand. The backyard is satisfied, the earth is satisfied. The fever breaks and I feel a surge of energy, as if it were not just time to rinse the day's coffee cups and put them in the dishwasher, but the beginning of the world.

Wavelength

A woman across the street waves.
Passing headlights splash across the sidewalk,
my eyes blur in the glare,
and the waving woman becomes a constellation
of women waving.
A man blows his nose into his hand;
the moon's bright fingers reach down
and touch him on the cheek.
Spiders of shadow skitter
as dawn kindles behind the east hills.
The sky turns the color of possibility,
and the world brims with seeing.

I read once that if I would only stop searching
for phrases, stop chasing after words,
and just turn the light inward,
my body-mind would, of itself,
drop-off, and my original face would appear.
But when I turned the light inward,
I saw only that I was unfinished,
a rough stone in an untilled field.
Wondering what would become
of me, I held my future
up to the light, but saw only flies
gathering over the field.

I have concluded that life is more likely based
on some statistically improbable series of numbers,
perhaps a punishment for thinking we humans might be noble
or grand, or have some purpose,
or just for thinking, period.

Meanwhile, the stones, the field and the flies,
the women, the man, the street,
the constellations, all turn,
first to dust, then to light,
and finally, waving, into nothing.

The Hero Becomes Acquainted with the Vagaries of Things

Sitting in bed
browsing on my laptop

I am enveloped in a cloud
of pale simulacra.

The morning grows sinister,
heavy with knowledge.

The new day gathers, sword in hand—
decisions everywhere, seeds within seeds,

no within yes, a bender,
everything occurring at once.

My thoughts, which once had something
of a firm, intelligent shape, blur, darken.

Tender people I knew growing up
burst into flames.

Old men drum their fingers,
and speak in dry voices of vanished jewels,

of shoes left along the roadside,
and other indignities.

I read an article about microplastics in our brains.
Apparently, five bottle caps worth, more or less.

Is this the life we planned, of cherry pie, of speckled light,
of knives and forks at the ready?

It seems the world has tired
of keeping promises.

Early morning traffic wobbles by outside.
The future hovers above, watching.

Necrophilous

Everything in life
slowly but surely changes
all of a sudden,

which makes me think a lot
about death,
which is distressing,

but I’ve also found
that it can be relaxing
to feel posthumous.

Universal Instructions

Choose a time when you're not rushed
or likely to be interrupted.

Follow these instructions precisely.
Do not attempt to install if pregnant.

Now that you have opened the box,
you can see all the parts organized in numbered bundles.

If you see a bundle numbered 17, you have made a mistake.
Put the parts back in the box and start over.

Whenever possible, the automated method should be employed to avoid joint pain. And remember,
Dum vita est, spes est.
To keep the operation simple, the timer settings can be easily overruled by altering the last programmed command.

Do not eat for 16 hours prior,
do not take more of it,
do not take it more often,
and do not take it for a longer time.

Fill a bowl or sink with warm water,
confirm your internet signal is stable and strong.

Wash your hands and wipe the area clean.
Velvet gloves are recommended.

Trim your hair to ¼ inch, sterilize all utensils, add ice to the shaker, and do not begin until the temperature indicator is green.

You may have your shirt on or off. If twitching occurs,
rub with a mixture of herbs and kosher salt.

Allow your breath to breathe itself. This helps the gasses reach all parts of the body and penetrate the appendix.

If you do not have an appendix, please
call the toll-free customer service number on the box.

Sit in front of a mirror, take the lid off, and tip your head back.
Pull down your lower eyelid, and look up and to the right.

When you've finished, stand close to the person you'd most like
to impress and see if they notice the difference.

Postures of Waking Up

I

Morning sashays in under a rosé sky
as if returning from a long absence, or
from a recurring dream, or, more likely, from a dream
that just doesn't matter anymore.
Two pigeons land on the windowsill,
lean together, as if whispering to each other.

II

I sit at the kitchen table in my pjs
drinking a cup of strong coffee,
eating a piece of toast with apricot jam.
Today, along with my morning brew,
pictures in the news of bony lips, black and green,
of children gassed in war,
eyes staring, blue tongues lolling.

III

The world never stops flexing its muscles.
I feel my heart pulsing in its grip
as the pictures in the paper take my will away;
I feel them leaking into my bloodstream.
Dragging my muddled self up from the table,
I knock my coffee cup to the shattering floor.
The pigeons fly off, the sky flies off,
the silence pours over me like a syrup.

Goodbye, Ice Cream

Late fading light,
clouds flying by,
a gentle breeze
stirs the leaves.
Beneath the tree,
a tearful girl
with tiny fingers
touches her hair,
her prom dress
in her closet,
her first child
in her belly.
A mourning dove
dives, rises, purrs
its spare melody.
Turning, looking up,
a child herself,
she hums along.

Biding, Abiding

Waiting for the evening
to give a little,
for the echo of human sounds to quiet,
the past rises-up in waves—

father in the far corner of the living room
making a pitcher of martinis,
my old paint horse in the open field below the house,
her tail dusting the ground,
my aunt wrapped in a blanket
reaching out for something only she could see—

memories I never expected to live
so long, so far beyond their moment,
shimmy and glint like a school of little fish
in the half-light of recollection,
even as the present, brusque and omnivorous,
swallows them up, one by one.

The Abyss

Late in life, sleep is a challenge.
It's best to establish a routine—
it helps to quit reading editorials before bed.
Better to drink Irish whisky;
the whisky makes your bedroom smell like church.
Also, be sure to make room for your dog on your bed.
My own dog curls-up at the foot of my bed,
forepaws as in prayer, which gets me thinking
maybe I should pray more. After all,
only a benevolent God
could conjure a dog curled-up,
forepaws as in prayer.
As I near the end of life,
I notice I am thinking more about God,
but even more about sleep.

Enlightenment

I couldn't see it.
Not in the old church,
not from the balcony in the September starlight.

After the holidays, I tried again,
but no.

You asked why not,
and I explained, disguising my explanation
as silence.

In the red bathroom,
the faucet dripping,
I could only stare, wordless, at the mirror.

Even in the palace of crystal,
the light framing the dancers,
I was blind to it.

I wanted to see it, I wanted to and wanted to,
until my wanting
wore itself out,

and I just lay down,
here on the sand among the dry rocks.

I just
lay
down,

and, as a flurry of finches swept up through the bare branches,
my eyes dropped away, and
I saw it.

No, it was not heroic or bigger than life,
nor was it mystical,
as I thought it would be.

It was just itself,
and I saw it.

Once, in a Small Patch of Sky

I saw once,
in a small patch
of sky
between buildings,
a great stillness.
I sometimes think about that.
And I think sometimes
about my friendship with my dog,
his pawprints in the wet sand,
and sometimes about a man I saw only once,
picking up acorns,
homemade tattoos on the backs of his hands.
And I often think about my mother,
how I walked past a long succession of rooms
at the crematorium
until I saw her body
lying there
in her new reality,
her face pale, slightly blue.
After a long silence,
they announced it was time
to wheel her into the furnace,

and in that moment,
sunlight entered the room
and kissed her on the crown of her head,
ever so gently.
When finally she left,
she was accompanied by clouds.

Coco Is at Home

My friend is sick.
I visit her in the hospital.
She says they still haven't found the source
of the bleeding.

She asks me,
Is this my final illness?

I feel the space between us widen.
I don't know. Maybe.
She says, *We're all just one diagnosis away, cariño.*

Later, she tells me that her dog, Coco, is at home
needing attention—a walk, feeding.
I'll take care of it.

I pour a cup of kibble into Coco's bowl.
Coco looks at it, sniffs it, steps away,
lies down, looks up at me.

At the market, I buy a quarter pound of ground beef.
Coco eats it all.

According to my friend, Coco is an emotional support dog,
an animal that provides comfort and companionship
to individuals with mental distress.

I could use such an animal.
Likewise, Coco.

Balancing Act

Smokey the Bear is well paid
for appearing in TV commercials,
but he is required to wear pants—
a punishing embarrassment for a bear.
It's hard not to feel sorry for him.
On the other hand,
Smokey has told countless children
only they can prevent forest fires,
a burden they will carry
for the rest of their lives.

Between the Stones

Often, when I'm first to wake up,
I pause in the bedroom doorway
and watch her sleep,
trace the bare movements of her muscles
where her shoulders marry her arms.
Her hair, half-lit, glimmers
in the sliver of sunlight the curtains allow,
her breath fluttering like a brook
when a fish swims through.

We are both well acquainted
with the wounds that come
with love, their weight and machinery.
Nonetheless, in the heat of it,
deep within love's house full of spiders,
we find a steadfast symmetry—

the dreams she offers, her belief in astrology
and in the healing power of prayer,
how her hair falls down her back,
how I like to talk about cars,
her precision, my ramble,
how she's sweetened,
unlike my tendency to be increasingly grumpy.

Outside, morning gains form—
an exuberant sky, rows of palms, swanky clouds,
and the scent of orange blossoms.
In the yard, birds, yellow and black,
peck for edibles between the stones,
insects swarm in a corridor of sunshine.

I tilt my head and fix my eyes on the sky.
Love follows its own vague laws,
shadows paint the shaded street beyond our wall
as the wind turns the clouds.
I see her image there, too, in the bright clouds—
in the kitchen making waffles
in her flannel pajamas,
filling the bird feeders in the yard—
until, finally, she dissolves into the light.

Dirt Road

We walk the old dirt road,
a road we've watched decay for years,

kicking-up dust
that settles in our hair.

The dust makes us look old,
she says, and as we stroll

we talk about things
we've lost, little things that have come

to stand for bigger things, talk
about what we want still,

about the grief of parting
and the cramp of reunion,

about how abundance and sorrow
can feel so much alike,

walking in the sun's late rays
under the weight of the dust.

Kismet

Let Hercules himself do what he may,
The cat will mew, and dog will have his day.
—Shakespeare, "Hamlet"

Every dog will have his day,
and every man
will have his day of feeling
like an over-ripe pear
that's fallen on the floor,

and every woman many days of feeling
something very heavy
has fallen onto her.

Every rustle will have its urgency,
every swollen hand its fist
and fist its pounding table,
every rage its cadence, every lie its pedestal.

Some girls will have their days
of wide-brimmed hats,
most will not.

Chiaroscuro

Night rubs its eyes, becomes dawn.
Thoughts scurry by in half-light
like snippets of mumbled speech
overheard on the street.
I can't stop them,
can't keep up with them,
combining, recombining.

> *What happens when we die?*
> *I've never owned a compass.*
> *What was the name of that bakery?*

Out now into the boundless space
that is daylight, light on top of light,
on top of light.
Buildings take on color,
their luminous geometries,
burgundy, onyx, silver,
combining, recombining.

> *Apparently, trees talk to each other*
> *What was our address when we lived in Vancouver?*

The light dwindles,
thin clouds,
so many ill friends.

My wife believes we're re-born
after we die,
life after life,
combining, recombining.
I do not. Of course,
I'm only guessing.

> *How old was Barry when he died?*
> *It's Rolling Pin. Rolling Pin Bakery.*

The Week in Review

Monday

Winter, five a.m.,
awake with one eye open
I'm almost human.

Tuesday

Rain falling silver,
the drops rolling down my cheek,
whispering her name.

Wednesday

The yard surrenders,
overgrown with question marks.
An old man's landscape.

Thursday

A soft wind flutters,
alders wave their frail branches,
I will soon be dead.

Friday

The afternoon grows
excited about itself:
a dozen crayons!

Saturday

Copper saxophones,
the mice dance on the table,
and beckon their friends.

Sunday

Next week lies in wait,
one by one the stars go out,
worn down by meaning.

As if the Dead Were Lurking Nearby

I am frightened
by the sun's expansion
and by a feeling the world is composed
only of parts that endlessly fail
to comprise a whole—
points, lines, edges, light,
all dominoes, dust, and contingency.
When I close my eyes in the dark,
I sense the dead lurking nearby,
hear their breathing
in the wind in the palms, their weeping
for loved ones lost in wars.
Even as the day's details brighten—
pale leaves on the sidewalk scattered
as if with some eternal purpose,
a sky dressed in grace, and a sense of the hand
of a gleaming deity just out of reach—
even then, I feel the pull
of the fathomless dark
and the outstretched arms
of the dead.

Report from the Afterlife

At first, you won't speak the language,
so things might feel a bit unstable,

but don't worry,
the announcer is always in a good mood.

And there's no penitential regime,
no hard facts, no prudish accounting.

Every afternoon, a cocktail combo plays lavender music
while people sit under lilacs and simply breathe.

Sound drizzles down through the air,
the melody modest but polished,

and the furnishings glow, lustrous drape of brocade,
foliage and beasts woven into the folds.

There are martinis and Chinese noodles,
the afterlife at its most relaxed.

As to your identity, pearls
against a white dress.

About the Author

Peter Schireson grew up in California, earned a B.A. from UC Berkeley, an M.Ed. at University of Victoria, and an Ed.D. from Harvard University. After retiring from a career, first in education and later in business, he returned to school to earn an MFA in Poetry from The Program for Writers at Warren Wilson College.

In addition to poems in journals, he has published four chapbooks, *The Welter of Me and You, The Salt, What Worlds and Moons,* and *Before the Sun*; and two full-length collections of poems, *Sword of Glass* (Broadstone Books) and *How We Met* (Kelsay Books).

He is an ordained Zen Buddhist priest, having trained in both the US and Japan. He is married to the psychologist and Zen teacher Grace Jill Schireson with whom he co-edited *Zen Bridge: The Zen Teachings of Keido Fukushima.*

Peter and Jill live in Palm Springs, California.

Website:
www.peterschireson.com

www.ingramcontent.com/pod-product-compliance
Lightning Source LLC
LaVergne TN
LVHW091813110826
845146LV00006B/1167

9798901468210